TABLE OF CONTE

MW00930596

Chapter 1: Introduction

- Brief overview of the movie "Shutter Island" (2010) directed by Martin Scorsese

The film "Shutter Island" (2010) masterfully unfolds under the direction of Martin Scorsese, taking audiences on a gripping and psychologically charged cinematic experience. In this brief introduction, we delve into the captivating world of this psychological thriller, exploring its compelling storyline, intricate characters, and haunting atmosphere. As viewers embark on the enthralling journey that "Shutter Island" presents, they are confrontiled with the fundamental questions of sanity, identity, and reality.

"Shutter Island" opens with the arrival of two U. S. marshals, Teddy Daniels (Leonardo DiCaprio) and Chuck Aule (Mark Ruffalo), to the mysterious and isolated Ashecliffe Hospital on Shutter Island. The plot immediately hooks the audience with its enigmatic premise, as Teddy investigates the disappearance of a patient from the hospital. The island's uncanny and foreboding atmosphere, emphasized by Scorsese's masterful cinematography and haunting soundtrack, sets the stage for a suspenseful exploration of the human psyche. From the very beginning, the film thrusts viewers into a world of uncertainty and murkiness, ensuring their undivided attention throughout the ensuing narrative.

As the plot continues to unravel, Scorsese masterfully reveals Teddy's backstory, a troubled past clouded by the death of his wife in a horrific arson fire. This personal trauma shapes Teddy's motivations as he delves deeper into the mysteries of Ashecliffe Hospital. His own inner demons and psychological struggle, which Leonardo DiCaprio so skillfully portrays, beckon the audience to question the reliable nature of his perceptions and judgements. The deep emotional wounds Teddy carries become not only a driving force for his character but also a captivating exploration of the fragility of the human mind.

In a film rife with breathtaking twists and intricacies, Martin Scorsese delivers a jaw-dropping finale that challenges all preconceived notions and pushes the boundaries of viewer expectations. As the truth surrounding the disappearance on Shutter Island is finally unveiled, audiences are thrown into an unexpected and disorienting sequence of events. Scorsese's expert storytelling technique forces audiences to grapple with the enigmatic nature of truth and the malleability of human perception.

Beyond the enthralling storyline and expertly crafted suspense, "Shutter Island" delves into profound psychological themes with deftness and gravity. The film prompts audiences to examine the nature of mental illness, the complexities of memory and trauma, and the morality surrounding the treatment of those deemed "insane. " Through the lens of Teddy's investigation, Scorsese explores the darker corners of the human psyche, asking viewers to ponder the nature of sanity and the resilience of the human spirit.

"Shutter Island" (2010) stands as a testament to Martin Scorsese's unparalleled storytelling and directorial prowess. Through the exceptional performances of its cast and a meticulously crafted narrative, this psychological thriller offers a truly riveting cinematic experience. By skillfully unraveling the layers of intrigue and blurring the lines between reality and illusion, Scorsese invites viewers into a world that challenges their perceptions and leaves an indelible mark on their psyche

- Introduce the themes explored in the movie

The movie Shutter Island, directed by the legendary Martin Scorsese, is truly a masterpiece that delves into the depths of the human mind.

Released in 2010, this psychological thriller takes the audience on a haunting journey filled with intrigue, suspense, and ultimately, a profound exploration of various themes. In this essay, we will unravel the deeply profound themes that Scorsese explores in Shutter Island, leaving no stone unturned as we dissect the intricacies of this cinematic gem.

One of the key themes explored in Shutter Island is the concept of identity. The movie presents us with a protagonist, U. S. Marshal Teddy Daniels, brilliantly portrayed by Leonardo DiCaprio, who is called upon to investigate the mysterious disappearance of a patient at Ashecliffe Hospital for the Criminally Insane. As Teddy delves deeper into the investigation, he begins to question his own sanity and grapple with his own troubled past. Throughout the film, Scorsese employs different narrative techniques, such as flashbacks and dream sequences, to challenge the viewer's perception of reality. This ambiguity surrounding identity creates a sense of unease and forces the audience to question their own understanding of the world, blurring the lines between sanity and madness.

Another prominent theme in Shutter Island is the power of manipulation. As Teddy explores the asylum, he encounters various characters who appear to be complicit in a larger conspiracy. It becomes apparent that the doctors and staff at Ashecliffe are engaged in unethical practices, using their knowledge of psychology to manipulate and control the minds of their patients. Scorsese expertly weaves this theme throughout the film, drawing parallels between the manipulation occurring within the walls of the institution and the larger societal structures of power and control. The viewer is forced to confront the unsettling idea that those in authority may wield their power to twist reality and shape the truth to suit their own agendas.

Additionally, Shutter Island raises questions about the nature of guilt and redemption. Teddy, burdened by the guilt of his wife's tragic death, becomes entangled in a web of conspiracy and self-discovery. Throughout the film, he seeks absolution for the sins of his past, wrestling with his own internal demons and attempting to come to terms with the choices he has made. This exploration of guilt and redemption taps into a timeless and universal human struggle, forcing the audience to confront their own capacity for forgiveness and self-forgiveness.

Furthermore, the movie explores the theme of perception versus reality. As Teddy investigates the disappearance of the patient, he is confronted with a series of mind-bending twists and turns, making it difficult for him (and the audience) to decipher what is real and what is imagined. The line between truth and deception is continuously blurred, challenging the viewer's perception of the events unfolding on screen. Scorsese expertly crafts an atmosphere of constant doubt and uncertainty, highlighting the notion that perception is a fragile and easily manipulated construct. Through its exploration of themes such as identity, manipulation, guilt, redemption, and perception versus reality, director Martin Scorsese has crafted a cinematic experience that leaves a lasting impact on its viewers. This compelling narrative forces us to question our own understanding of the world, blurring the lines between fiction and reality. Shutter Island is not just a film; it is a thought-provoking examination of the human condition and a testament to Scorsese's remarkable talent as a filmmaker

- Discuss the significance of the setting and time period

Shutter Island, directed by Martin Scorsese, is a cinematic masterpiece that delves deep into the realms of psychological intrigue and mystery. The setting and time period of the film play a crucial role in shaping the narrative and enhancing its overall impact. Scorsese pays immense attention to detail, meticulously recreating the 1950s ambience and the eerie island setting, both of which contribute significantly to the story's tone, atmosphere, and character development.

The significance of the setting, Shutter Island itself, can hardly be overstated. Nestled in the heart of the Boston Harbor, this isolated, foreboding island exudes a sense of confinement and isolation that is eminently palpable throughout the film. Its rocky shores and towering cliffs serve as a visual metaphor for the inner struggles and mental incarceration faced by the characters, particularly the protagonist, Teddy Daniels. The omnipresent presence of water, surrounding the island in its entirety, casts an air of secrecy and confinement, mirroring the inner turmoil and emotional entrapment that Teddy experiences as he unravels the haunting mysteries that lie within Ashcliffe Hospital.

Moreover, the time period in which the story is set, the 1950s, adds a layer of historical significance and context to the narrative. In this post-war era, the United States was grappling with the aftermath of World War II, McCarthyism, and the emergence of the Cold War. Scorsese skillfully weaves these historical elements into the fabric of the story, heightening the sense of paranoia, mistrust, and uncertainty that permeates Shutter Island. The conservative political climate of the time, coupled with the prevailing notion of conformity and strict social norms, mirror the oppressive nature of

Ashcliffe Hospital and the deliberate silencing and suppression of uncomfortable truths throughout the film.

Furthermore, the 1950s were a period marked by significant advancements in the field of psychiatry. The nascent developments in mental health treatment during this time greatly influenced the narrative of Shutter Island. Scorsese masterfully utilizes this setting to explore the evolving ideologies surrounding mental illness and the questionable ethical boundaries that often accompanied experimental psychiatric practices. The prevalence of lobotomies and other controversial treatments during this era adds to the unease and discomfort experienced by the audience, effectively blurring the line between reality and delusion in Teddy's quest for truth.

The attention to detail in recreating the 1950s era is evident in every aspect of the film's design, from the costumes and production design to the meticulous set construction. This attention to historical accuracy not only lends authenticity to the film but also serves as a narrative tool, enhancing the atmosphere and immersing the audience in Teddy's increasingly distorted perception of reality. The dark, moody cinematography and the hauntingly evocative score further contribute to the overall immersive experience, transporting the viewer to a bygone era rife with tension, uncertainty, and psychological distress. Martin Scorsese's attention to detail in recreating the eerie island setting and historical context of the 1950s enriches the narrative, deepens the psychological intrigue, and enhances the film's overall impact. The oppressive and isolated atmosphere of Shutter Island parallels the mental struggles faced by the characters, while the historical context amplifies the themes of paranoia and uncertainty. Through his masterful storytelling, Scorsese transports the audience into a world where reality and delusion intermingle, leaving a lasting impression long after the credits roll

Chapter 2: Plot Summary

- *Provide a detailed synopsis of the plot*

The plot revolves around the enigmatic protagonist, U. S. Marshal Teddy Daniels, who finds himself trapped in the unsettling Ashecliffe Hospital for the Criminally Insane located on Shutter Island.

The story begins with Teddy and his new partner, Chuck Aule, being assigned to investigate the mysterious disappearance of patient Rachel Solando, a convicted murderess who seemingly vanished from her locked cell in the secured facility. As they arrive on the island, the duo becomes increasingly unnerved by the foreboding atmosphere pervading Ashecliffe Hospital.

As Teddy delves deeper into the investigation, he begins to experience vivid flashbacks and nightmares related to his own traumatic past, particularly his service as a U. S. Army soldier liberating the Dachau concentration camp during World War II. These haunting memories haunt him, further blurring the lines between reality and illusion.

Suspicions arise when Teddy encounters seemingly obstructive behavior from the staff and uncooperative patients at Ashecliffe Hospital. He discovers a series of experiments performed on individuals, including the administration of psychotropic drugs and lobotomies, which raises troubling ethical questions about the hospital's practices. Soon, Teddy finds himself caught in a labyrinth of deception, unsure whom to trust and whether the malevolent forces at play on Shutter Island are external or internal.

As the plot thickens, Teddy's search intensifies, leading him to Dr. Cawley, the enigmatic head psychiatrist at Ashecliffe Hospital. Taking an unconventional approach, Teddy infiltrates the inner workings of the facility to unravel the truth. Paranoia and suspense escalate as he uncovers a secretive plot regarding the manipulation of selected patients, known as the "kites," to root out a former patient turned murderous escapee, Andrew Laeddis.

Ultimately, Teddy unravels the devastating truth that has been hidden from him throughout his investigation. He realizes that he himself is actually Andrew Laeddis and that Ashecliffe Hospital has been employing an elaborate role-playing therapy to help him confront his guilt over the tragic deaths of his wife Dolores Chanal and their three children. The hospital staff, including Dr. Cawley, played various roles to push Teddy into acknowledging his true identity.

This shocking twist challenges everything the audience thought they knew about Teddy's journey and raises existential questions about the nature of reality, identity, and the limits of the human psyche. By interweaving Teddy's personal trauma with the complex web of deceit on Shutter Island, Scorsese crafts a psychological thriller that leaves the audience questioning their own perceptions and moral compass. With its commendable attention to detail, the film successfully captivates the viewer with its psychological complexities, thrilling suspense, and thought-provoking exploration of the human psyche

- Analyze the characters and their motivations

The complex narrative and psychological aspects of the film provide the perfect canvas to examine the inner workings of the characters and understand their underlying motivations. Let us delve into the depths of Shutter Island to unravel the enigmatic personas that drive the plot forward.

At the heart of Shutter Island is the character of Teddy Daniels, portrayed brilliantly by Leonardo DiCaprio. Teddy, a U. S. Marshal, is depicted as a tormented soul, haunted by the demons of his past.

Clad in emotional scars, his motivations are fueled by a desire for justice and redemption. As he investigates the disappearance of a patient from Ashecliffe Hospital, Teddy's personal experiences as a World War II veteran intertwine with the case, blurring the lines between reality and illusion. His psychological journey becomes a means for him to confront his own traumas and seek closure. Teddy's unwavering determination to uncover the truth is driven by his need to face the demons that have tormented him for far too long.

In contrast, Dr. Cawley, played by Ben Kingsley, presents a character with motivations shrouded in mystery. As the psychiatrist in charge of Ashecliffe Hospital, he exudes an air of professional confidence and authority. However, as the plot progresses, it becomes evident that Dr. Cawley is hiding crucial information from Teddy. Although his motivations initially appear to be in conflict with Teddy's quest for truth, it is revealed that Dr. Cawley is not entirely devoid of compassion and empathy. His actions, driven by a desire to protect his patients, challenge the viewer's perception of his character, adding a layer of complexity to the plot.

Another intriguing character is Rachel Solando, portrayed by Emily Mortimer. She serves as the catalyst for Teddy's investigation, as her disappearance sets the events of the film in motion. Rachel's motivations, carefully crafted to keep the audience guessing, present a puzzling conundrum. Her initial disappearance from the mental institution suggests a desire to escape the horrors within. However, as the layers of the plot unfold, it becomes apparent that nothing is as it seems. Rachel's motivations become entwined with the enigmatic web of the plot, leaving the viewer questioning her true intentions and rationale.

Furthermore, the character of Chuck Aule, played by Mark Ruffalo, plays a vital role in Teddy's quest for the truth. As Teddy's partner, Chuck's motivations become entangled with the mysteries of Ashecliffe Hospital. While initially presented as a loyal and trustworthy companion, his true intentions remain murky throughout the film. The revelation of

Chuck's ultimate motivations adds a unique twist to the narrative, challenging our perception of his character and leaving room for multiple interpretations.

In analyzing the characters and their motivations in Shutter Island, it becomes clear that the plot hinges on the delicate balance between reality and fantasy. The characters, each layered with their own psychological complexities, add depth to the storyline. Teddy's pursuit of justice, Dr. Cawley's need to protect his patients, Rachel's ambiguous motivations, and Chuck's hidden agenda all contribute to the suspenseful atmosphere of the film.

As the film progresses, the motivations of each character are peeled back like layers of an onion, revealing hidden depths and unforeseen truths. This intricate dance between revelation and deception keeps the audience engaged, questioning the authenticity of every character and the intentions that drive them forward. As Teddy Daniels embarks on a journey to unravel the mysteries of Ashecliffe

Hospital, the motivations of each character are unveiled, challenging the viewer's perception and adding depth to the already intriguing storyline. Through their complex motivations, the characters in Shutter Island exemplify the psychological depths explored within the film, making it a masterclass in psychological thrillers

- Examine the key events that drive the storyline

These events serve as crucial plot points that not only propel the narrative forward but also deeply impact the psychological and emotional state of the characters.

One of the pivotal events in the film is the arrival of U. S. Marshal Teddy Daniels and his partner Chuck Aule to Shutter Island. Their purpose is to investigate the disappearance of Rachel Solando, a patient from the Ashecliffe Hospital, a facility for the criminally insane. This sets the foundation for the storyline and establishes the primary goal for the protagonists - to uncover the truth behind Solando's disappearance.

As the investigation progresses, Teddy's psychological state begins to unravel due to his own haunted past and the eerie atmosphere of the island. This is exemplified by his recurring flashbacks of his experiences in World War II and the tragic death of his wife Dolores. These events serve as driving factors for Teddy's emotional turbulence, leading him to question his own sanity and making the audience question the reliability of the events unfolding on screen.

Another significant event in the storyline is Teddy's encounter with Dr. Cawley, the head psychiatrist at Ashecliffe Hospital. Throughout their conversations, there is a constant sense of tension and suspicion. Driven by his determination to uncover the dark secrets of the hospital, Teddy begins to challenge Dr. Cawley's explanations, suspecting a conspiracy is at play. This confrontation not only adds depth to Teddy's character but also raises questions about the true nature of the hospital and its involvement in unethical activities.

The plot takes a dramatic turn when Teddy and Chuck discover a hidden underground facility on the island. Here, they stumble upon evidence that suggests illegal human experimentation, involving mind control and lobotomies, are taking place. This revelation further escalates the suspense and heightens the stakes for the protagonists, as their belief in the integrity of the hospital is shattered.

One of the most shocking events in the storyline is the revelation of Teddy's true identity. It is revealed that he is actually Andrew Laeddis, a former patient at Ashecliffe Hospital who was admitted after he killed his wife in a fit of rage. This twist not only subverts the audience's expectations but also forces a reevaluation of all the events that have transpired so far. It becomes clear that Teddy's investigation and all the events on Shutter Island are actually a part of an elaborate roleplay orchestrated by the hospital staff as an attempt to bring about a breakthrough in his treatment for mental illness.

The climax of the film occurs when Teddy, now fully embracing his true identity as Andrew Laeddis, decides to confront Dr. Cawley. In a shocking turn of events, he realizes that the doctors want him to perform one final act - to lobotomize himself as a means of escaping his painful memories and guilt. This desperate and climactic event, driven by Andrew's desire to regain control over his own mind and actions, effectively concludes the storyline with a haunting and tragic resolution. From Teddy's arrival to Shutter Island, to the unraveling of the truth behind the hospital's activities, and culminating in a shocking revelation of his true identity, these events propel the plot forward while also facilitating a deep exploration of themes such as guilt, deception, and the boundaries of sanity. They are pivotal moments that engage audiences and cement "Shutter Island" as a gripping and thought-provoking psychological thriller

Chapter 3: Tone and Atmosphere

- Explore the dark and suspenseful tone of the movie

In the realm of psychological thrillers, few films can match the intense and disquieting atmosphere that permeates Martin Scorsese's masterpiece, Shutter Island (2010). As we explore this crucial element, a sense of foreboding envelops us, and we are compelled to unravel the psychological labyrinth that unfolds before our eyes.

From the opening scenes of Shutter Island, Scorsese thrusts us into a world shrouded in darkness and mystery. The bleak and isolated landscape of the island, with its imposing cliffs and desolate shores, sets the stage for the ominous events that are about to unfold. The director's masterful use of stark and contrasting lighting enhances the suspense, casting long shadows and generating an air of unease in every frame. Through the interplay of light and shadow, Scorsese masterfully manipulates our emotions, heightening our senses and evoking a constant state of apprehension.

Moreover, the narrative structure of Shutter Island further contributes to its dark and suspenseful tone. The film follows the investigation of two U. S. Marshals, Teddy Daniels and Chuck Aule, as they search for a missing patient from Ashecliffe Hospital, a facility for the criminally insane. As the marshals delve deeper into the heart of the island, they encounter devious mind games and obscure clues, each step unveiling pieces of a sinister puzzle. The non-linear progression of the story not only adds complexity but also serves to disorient and disturb the viewer, mirroring the psychological turmoil experienced by the characters themselves.

Scorsese employs a range of cinematic techniques to heighten the suspense throughout Shutter Island. The eerie and haunting musical score by Robbie Robertson establishes an atmosphere of tension and impending doom. It pulses beneath the surface, evoking an unshakeable feeling of unease. The precise and deliberate pacing of the film also contributes to the overall claustrophobic ambiance, as the audience is forced to sit on the edge of their seats, anxious to uncover the truth that lies hidden within the layers of deception.

The mise-en-scène of Shutter Island further amplifies its dark and suspenseful tone. Scorsese meticulously crafts a visual world that exudes a sense of palpable dread. The dilapidated and decaying settings of the asylum speak to the deteriorating mental state of its inhabitants, while the rooms and corridors are dressed in oppressive ornamental details, symbolic of the psychological labyrinth the characters find themselves trapped within. The overwhelming presence of water throughout the film - be it in the form of rain, mist, or the raging sea - adds to the sense of confinement and impending catastrophe. Scorsese effectively harnesses these elements to thrust the audience further into the depths of darkness and despair.

Ultimately, it is the magnetic performances of the cast that solidify the dark and suspenseful atmosphere in Shutter Island. Leonardo DiCaprio's portrayal of Teddy Daniels is nothing short of mesmerizing. His nuanced performance captures the character's internal struggle and descent into madness with an intensity that is both captivating and unsettling. The supporting cast, including Mark Ruffalo, Ben Kingsley, and Michelle Williams, further contribute to the film's dark tone, delivering gripping performances that leave the audience on edge throughout. Through his masterful use of lighting, narrative structure, cinematic techniques, mise-en-scène, and stellar performances, Scorsese immerses us in a world of paranoia and uncertainty. As viewers, we are captivated by the film's foreboding atmosphere, compelled to unravel its deep-rooted mysteries. Shutter Island is a testament to Scorsese's ability to craft a chilling and unforgettable cinematic experience

- Discuss how the atmosphere contributes to the overall mood

The atmosphere of a film plays a crucial role in setting the overall mood and enhancing the viewing experience. In the case of "Shutter Island," directed by Martin Scorsese, the atmosphere is meticulously crafted to contribute to the psychological thriller's eerie and suspenseful mood. By employing a range of techniques such as lighting, sound design, and production design, Scorsese effectively creates an unsettling and foreboding atmosphere throughout the film, leaving the audience feeling deeply unsettled and engrossed in the unfolding mystery.

One of the primary ways the atmosphere contributes to the overall mood of "Shutter Island" is through the masterful use of lighting. In particular, the film employs a dark and shadowy lighting scheme that helps to create an ominous and mysterious atmosphere. Shadows dominate the majority of the scenes, enveloping the characters and amplifying the sense of impending danger. This use of lighting not only adds to the film's sense of unease but also symbolizes the blurred line between reality and illusion, a recurring theme in the film.

The utilization of sound design also plays a significant role in establishing the haunting atmosphere in "Shutter Island. " Throughout the film, the soundtrack is punctuated by eerie, discordant noises and unsettling music, effectively creating a sense of tension and anticipation. Scorsese expertly employs sound as a means of conveying the characters' unease and disorientation, amplifying the psychological aspect of the thriller genre. The sound consistently contributes to the overall mood, keeping the audience on edge and emphasizing the intense psychological experience of the characters.

Furthermore, the production design of "Shutter Island" greatly enhances the atmospheric mood. The isolated and desolate setting of the titular island adds to the film's sense of unease and confinement. The imposing cliffs, tumultuous sea, and oppressive weather create a feeling of isolation for the characters, intensifying the overall mood of the film. By choosing a location that emphasizes their isolation and vulnerability, Scorsese effectively adds to the suspense and sense of impending doom that permeates throughout "Shutter Island. ".

In addition to lighting, sound design, and production design, the choice of color palette also contributes to the overall atmosphere of the film. The predominantly cool and desaturated color scheme further enhances the bleak and unsettling mood of "Shutter Island. " The absence of vibrant colors reinforces the characters' sense of despair and highlights the sinister undertones present throughout the narrative. This deliberate choice of color scheme effectively immerses the audience in the world of the film, allowing them to experience the psychological torment endured by the characters. Through the skillful use of lighting, sound design, production design, and color palette, director Martin Scorsese creates an unsettling and foreboding atmosphere that submerges the audience into a world of fear and uncertainty. By carefully employing these techniques, Scorsese ensures that the atmosphere remains consistent throughout, leaving the viewers captivated and enveloped in the enigmatic story

- Examine the use of symbolism and imagery in creating a sense of unease

The utilization of symbolism and imagery is an integral aspect of the film Shutter Island (2010), directed by the phenomenal Martin Scorsese. This essay will delve into the various techniques employed by Scorsese to heighten tension and instill a sense of disquiet in the audience's minds.

One example of potent symbolism in Shutter Island can be found in the recurrent presence of water throughout the film. Water, with its fluid and ever-changing nature, acts as a metaphor for the subconscious mind and the depth of the characters' psyches. This symbolism is evident in the frequent shots of turbulent waves crashing against the rocks, reflecting the tumultuous psychological state of the protagonist, Teddy Daniels. As the story progresses, these visuals become increasingly ominous, serving as a harbinger of the revelations that lie beneath the surface of the island.

Furthermore, the imagery of lighthouses in the film serves to further augment the prevailing sense of unease. Lighthouses traditionally represent guidance and safety, yet in Shutter Island, they take on a sinister connotation. The Beacon, an imposing lighthouse atop a cliff, overlooks the entire island and exudes an eerie glow in the night. This juxtaposition of light and darkness is key in creating an unsettling atmosphere, as it hints at the play between truth and deception throughout the narrative.

Scorsese also employs visual symbolism through the use of recurring motifs, such as the clocks that permeate the island's various settings. Clocks symbolize the passage of time and the ticking inevitability of our mortality. In Shutter Island, they are depicted as either frozen or ticking rapidly, emphasizing the characters' desperate attempts to hold on to their memories and maintain control over their lives. This subverts the familiar notion of time as a measure of solace, transforming it into a source of anxiety and foreboding.

Additionally, the powerful imagery captured in the depiction of isolated spaces on the island amplifies the sense of unease experienced by the characters and the viewers. The dilapidated and desolate buildings, surrounded by harsh and unforgiving cliffs, evoke a feeling of confinement and entrapment. These evocative visuals serve as physical manifestations of the characters' psychological states, mirroring their internal struggles and exacerbating the overall atmospheric tension.

In order to expand upon the atmosphere of unease, Scorsese adeptly utilizes cinematography techniques that visually enhance the symbolism and imagery present in the film. He employs a desaturated color palette, resulting in a visually sterile and cold environment. This aesthetic choice reflects the clinical nature of the institution and intensifies the disturbing atmosphere, as the muted colors seem drained of life and emotion. This deliberate stylistic decision creates a distance between the audience and the characters, further enhancing the unease and uncertainty that pervades the entire film.

Moreover, Scorsese leverages sound design to accentuate the sense of unease throughout the film. The dissonant and unsettling soundtrack adds an alarming layer of tension, perfectly complementing the visual elements. The deliberate use of jarring sounds, such as screeching violins and eerie whispers, amplifies the feeling of apprehension and heightens the overall sense of dread. Through the depiction of water, lighthouses, clocks, isolated spaces, and the employment of cinematography and sound design, Martin Scorsese effectively establishes a palpable atmosphere of tension and apprehension. The utilization of these techniques illuminates the characters' psychological turmoil and immerses the audience in an unsettling world where truth becomes elusive. Shutter Island stands as a testament to Scorsese's brilliance in crafting a psychological thriller that remains etched in the viewers' minds long after the credits roll

Chapter 4: Psychological Themes

- Analyze the psychological aspects of the film

Director Martin Scorsese skillfully crafts a gripping narrative that explores various psychological concepts, making the movie an intriguing journey into the human mind.

One of the primary psychological themes explored in Shutter Island is the nature of reality and perception. The film challenges the audience to question what is real and what is merely a construct of the protagonist's troubled mind. Teddy Daniels, brilliantly portrayed by Leonardo DiCaprio, is a U. S. Marshal investigating the disappearance of a patient in Ashecliffe Hospital for the Criminally Insane. As the story unfolds, Teddy's reality becomes increasingly distorted, blurring the lines between truth and delusion.

Scorsese carefully employs various cinematic techniques to enhance the audience's understanding of Teddy's psychological state. The frequent use of jump cuts, quick editing, and disorienting close-ups create a sense of unease, mimicking the fractured mental state Teddy experiences. Additionally, the incorporation of dream sequences further blurs the boundary between reality and fantasy, leaving the audience questioning the reliability of the information presented.

Another psychological aspect explored in Shutter Island is the theme of trauma and its impact on the human psyche. Teddy's own past trauma, related to his experiences as a soldier during World War II, serves as the catalyst for his descent into madness. The film suggests that traumatic experiences can have a profound and lasting effect on individuals, leading them to develop coping mechanisms or even alter their perception of reality.

Through meticulous character development, Scorsese showcases the complex nature of trauma and its consequences. Teddy's erratic behavior, his persistent flashbacks, and nightmares reveal the extent to which his past exploits haunt him. As the audience delves deeper into Teddy's psyche, it becomes apparent that the boundaries between sanity and insanity are precarious, highlighting the fragile nature of the human mind when faced with trauma.

Furthermore, the film Shutter Island delves into the theme of guilt and its psychological ramifications. All the characters, including Teddy himself, carry deep-seated feelings of guilt. This guilt is intricately interwoven with their perception of reality, leading them down a path of self-destruction.

Scorsese employs visual cues and symbolism to highlight the characters' guilt. For example, water consistently appears throughout the film, symbolizing guilt's ability to drown individuals in their own remorse. Teddy's visions of his dead wife, Dolores, and the reoccurring phrase "Why are you all wet, baby?" further emphasize the inescapable burden of guilt that the characters carry.

The psychological aspect of guilt is amplified through the use of unreliable narration. The audience is repeatedly led to believe in certain events or motives, only to have their expectations shattered by subsequent revelations. This manipulation of the narrative keeps the audience on edge, constantly questioning what is true and what is merely a figment of Teddy's tormented psyche. Director Martin Scorsese skillfully explores themes of reality and perception, trauma, and guilt, offering viewers a thought-provoking cinematic journey. Through the use of visual cues, symbolism, and unreliable narration, the film immerses the audience in a disorienting world where the lines between reality and fiction are blurred. By analyzing these psychological aspects, we gain a deeper understanding of the complex human psyche and the devastating effects of trauma and guilt. Shutter

Island stands as a testament to Scorsese's unparalleled ability to create a psychological thriller that challenges conventional storytelling, leaving audiences questioning their own perceptions of the world

- Discuss the themes of memory, trauma, and identity

In the psychological thriller "Shutter Island" (2010) directed by Martin Scorsese, themes such as memory, trauma, and identity serve as crucial elements that contribute to the gripping narrative. Through an analytical lens, this essay offers a comprehensive examination of memory, trauma, and identity, highlighting their profound impact on the characters and plot development.

Memory:.

Memory serves as a significant theme in "Shutter Island," driving the story forward and blurring the lines between reality and illusion. S. Marshal Teddy Daniels. Daniels' own recollections are frequently challenged throughout the film, leaving viewers uncertain about the reliability of his narrative. This uncertainty mirrors the fragility of memory itself, as it can be influenced by trauma and objective manipulation.

Trauma:.

Trauma plays a pivotal role in the film, shaping the narrative and causing psychological deterioration in several characters. Chapter 4 draws attention to the traumatic experiences endured by Daniels, which haunt him throughout the story. Scorsese skillfully portrays trauma as a catalyst for paranoia and mental disarray, forcing Daniels to confront his past traumas while investigating a chilling mystery. The portrayal of trauma in "Shutter Island" reminds viewers of the lasting impact such experiences can have on an individual's psyche, leading them to question the nature of reality.

Identity:.

Identity is a central theme seamlessly woven into the fabric of "Shutter Island," and Chapter 4 offers keen insights into its exploration. The blurring of identity is exemplified in Teddy Daniels' own quest for self-discovery, which is interwoven with the mysteries and secrets of the island. As the plot unfolds, the audience is forced to question the authenticity of Daniels' true identity, leaving room for doubt and uncertainty as to whether he is a reliable narrator or an unreliable character caught in his own web of delusion. Furthermore, the duality and shifting identities depicted in the film metaphorically represent the complexity of the human psyche.

Interplay between Memory, Trauma, and Identity:. The trauma experienced by Teddy Daniels informs his fragmented memory, creating a scenario where his own identity becomes uncertain. The erosion of his memory as a result of past events further fuels his trauma and challenges his understanding of self. Scorsese masterfully merges these themes to emphasize that memory and trauma are closely linked, shaping and reshaping one's identity. Scorsese's film adaptation masterfully incorporates these themes, leaving viewers with a profound sense of the intricate relationships between memory, trauma, and identity. By defying conventions and blurring the boundaries of reality, the film delves into the depths of the human mind, ultimately posing thought-provoking questions about the nature of memory, the influence of trauma, and the fragile construct of identity

- Explore how the characters grapple with their own perceptions of reality

Shutter Island, directed by Martin Scorsese in 2010, is a gripping psychological thriller that explores the intricacies of the human mind. Based on the book "Shutter Island: Unraveling the Psychological Thriller," the film delves into how the characters grapple with their own perceptions of reality. This essay examines the psychological themes of the film, primarily focusing on the characters' struggles to distinguish between truth and illusion. Through the masterful direction of Scorsese and the compelling performances of the cast, Shutter Island invites the audience to question their own perceptions of reality.

The film presents a diverse array of characters, each grappling with their own perceptions of reality. Teddy Daniels, played by Leonardo DiCaprio, serves as the film's protagonist. Daniels, an emotionally scarred U. S. Marshal, undergoes immense inner turmoil as he attempts to investigate the mysterious disappearance of a patient at Ashecliffe Mental Hospital on Shutter Island.

Throughout the film, Daniels' perceptions of reality become increasingly unstable. Haunted by his past experiences and tormented by traumatic memories, he battles with delusions, hallucinations, and a distorted sense of reality. His quest to uncover the truth is confounded by his own fragmented mind, leaving both the audience and Daniels questioning the authenticity of his surroundings.

Daniels' partner, Chuck Aule, portrayed by Mark Ruffalo, serves as a grounding force amidst the chaotic atmosphere. As the plot progresses, Aule also finds himself grappling with his own perception of reality. Together, Daniels and Aule embark on a journey that tests the boundaries between sanity and madness, constantly forcing them to confront the reliability of their own senses.

Psychological Themes:.

Shutter Island expounds upon several psychological themes that underscore the characters' struggles with reality. One such theme is the fragility of memory. The film emphasizes that memories are subjective constructs that can be altered and manipulated. Memories fusion, a process in which two or more memories are combined, blurs the line between real and imagined events for both the characters and the audience. This technique further accentuates the difficulty in discerning truth from fiction.

Moreover, the film delves into the concept of cognitive dissonance. The characters' perception of reality clashes with the objective truth, leading to a state of dissonance. They enter a psychological minefield where the need to make sense of their experiences clashes with the desire to uphold preconceived notions of the world. The film challenges the viewers to contemplate the profound effects of cognitive dissonance and its implications on individual perception.

Furthermore, the film explores the power of suggestion. Ashecliffe Mental Hospital utilizes various psychological techniques to control and manipulate the perceptions of its inhabitants. Through conditioning, hypnosis, and drugs, the characters' views of reality are disrupted, leaving them vulnerable to manipulation. This examination of suggestion raises pertinent questions about the nature of reality and the extent to which one's thoughts can be influenced.

Shutter Island, directed by Martin Scorsese, probes into the complex and fragmented nature of human perception. Through the experiences of its characters, particularly Teddy Daniels and Chuck Aule, the film forces the audience to confront the blurred lines of reality. The psychological themes of fragility of memory, cognitive dissonance, and the power of suggestion underscore the characters' internal struggles. By foregrounding these themes, Scorsese challenges our preconceived notions about the nature of reality and compels us to reconsider our own perceptions. Captivating and thought-provoking, Shutter Island invites us to question the very fabric of our existence and the thin line separating what is real from what is imagined

Chapter 5: Cinematic Techniques

- Examine the film's use of cinematography and visual effects

Martin Scorsese's psychological thriller, "Shutter Island" (2010), expertly delves into the human psyche, blurring the lines between reality and delusion. This essay will engage in a detailed analysis of key cinematic techniques utilized in this chapter, highlighting their significance in enhancing the film's suspense, atmosphere, and narrative.

1 - The Power of Lighting:.

The film employs lighting as a pivotal tool to create an eerie and foreboding atmosphere that mirrors the dark psyche of the characters. From the first frame, Scorsese uses low-key lighting, with shadows enveloping characters, casting doubts on their intentions and intensifying their enigmatic nature. For instance, in the scene where Teddy Daniels (played by Leonardo DiCaprio) investigates the lighthouse, a stark contrast in lighting is used to intensify the suspense. The dimly lit interiors and the flickering of the lone bulb imbue the scene with palpable tension, leaving the audience on the edge of their seats.

2 - Capturing Isolation and Paranoia:.

Scorsese employs framing and composition to effectively convey a sense of isolation and paranoia throughout the film. One example is the utilization of wide-angle shots that showcase the vast and desolate landscape of the island. These shots not only emphasize the physical isolation of the institution but also mirror the emotional isolation experienced by the main character, Teddy Daniels. The visual distortion caused by the wide-angle lens further adds to a disorientating effect on the audience, allowing them to delve deeper into Teddy's psychological dilemma.

3 - Symbolic Visuals and Metaphors:.

The film harnesses visual effects to convey symbolism and metaphoric images that reveal the underlying themes. An example of this lies in the recurring water imagery, particularly the stormy seas encircling the island. The crashing waves and relentless rain serve as a visual metaphor, representing the tumultuous and uncontrollable aspects of Teddy's subconscious mind. Through this imagery, the audience becomes enveloped in the same sense of confusion, constantly questioning the validity of Teddy's reality.

4 - Subtle Camera Movements and Dynamic Angles:.

Scorsese employs a range of camera movements and angles to manipulate the viewer's perception and intensify the emotional impact of the film. One notable technique is the use of the dolly zoom, also known as the "Vertigo effect," for key moments in the narrative. This technique involves zooming in while simultaneously moving the camera backward, creating a disorienting and unsettling sensation. A prime instance of this is in the scene where Teddy confronts Dr. Cawley (played by Ben Kingsley), where the dolly zoom amplifies Teddy's growing paranoia and psychological warfare. Through the expert use of lighting, framing, visual effects, and dynamic camera angles, Scorsese succeeds in creating an atmosphere shrouded in mystery and psychological turmoil. Each technique employed serves to heighten the tension, deepen the psychological complexity of the characters, and engross the audience into the unsettling world of "Shutter Island. " This captivating film reminds us of the profound impact film techniques can have on the viewer's emotional engagement, making it a truly exceptional exploration of the human psyche on the big screen

- Discuss the sound design and music score

Through their strategic use, the sound design and music score effectively contribute to the film's overall themes and amplify the impact of key scenes.

One aspect worth examining is the clever and skillful manipulation of ambient sounds in the film. Ambient sounds are the background noises that help to establish the film's setting and enhance its realism. For instance, the faint sound of waves crashing against the cliffs in the distance and the occasional gusts of wind serve to remind the audience of the island's remoteness and create an unsettling feeling of isolation.

Another noteworthy element is the use of non-diegetic music, specifically the film's original score composed by Robbie Robertson. The score functions as a potent tool in manipulating the emotional responses of the audience. For example, during key scenes such as Teddy's investigation of the lighthouse, the score intensifies, heightening the suspense and contributing to the eerie and foreboding atmosphere that surrounds him.

Furthermore, Scorsese adeptly employs diegetic music within the narrative, strategically placing familiar songs from the 1950s to trigger memories from Teddy's past. The inclusion of songs such as "This Bitter Earth" by Dinah Washington and "Foggy Mountain Breakdown" by Flatt & Scruggs not only create a nostalgic ambiance but also serve as significant plot devices.

The juxtaposition of sound design and music score is another key element in highlighting the psychological aspects of the film. Scorsese skillfully disrupts the traditional use of sound in certain sequences, creating a sense of distortion and disorientation for the audience. Silence is employed strategically in Chapter 5, heightening tension and creating an eerie counterpoint to moments of heightened sound. By intentionally disrupting the expected patterns of sound within the narrative, Scorsese successfully amplifies the protagonist's inner turmoil and contributes to the overall sense of unease. Through the utilization of ambience, both diegetic and non-diegetic music, and the manipulation of sound patterns, Martin Scorsese creates an unnerving atmosphere that engulfs the viewer in the psychological maze of Teddy Daniels' mind. By skillfully harnessing these cinematic techniques, the viewer becomes an active participant in deciphering the mysteries of Shutter Island, ultimately resulting in an unforgettable and immersive cinematic experience

- Explore how Scorsese's directing style enhances the storytelling

Scorsese's directing style in the film "Shutter Island" is nothing short of exceptional, and it greatly enhances the storytelling. Through his masterful use of various cinematic techniques, Scorsese succeeds in immersing the audience into the nightmarish world of the titular island. ".

One of Scorsese's key strengths lies in his ability to create a sense of unease and suspense through his use of visual symbolism. As he steps off the boat, Scorsese employs a low-angle shot to emphasize Teddy's vulnerability in a disorienting and ominous environment. This simple choice of camera angle immediately establishes a sense of unease, making the audience feel as though something is off. Through this visual technique, Scorsese effectively hooks the viewers and propels them further into the story.

In addition to visual symbolism, Scorsese expertly uses sound design to enhance the storytelling. Throughout the film, he employs a unique combination of non-diegetic and diegetic sounds to create a disorienting and unsettling atmosphere. Scorsese implements a mix of heavy breathing, distant screams, and eerie music to heighten the tension. This deliberate choice of sound design intensifies the sense of isolation and fear that Teddy experiences, and it also serves to immerse the audience even further into the psychological thriller aspect of the story.

Scorsese's innovative use of editing techniques is another aspect that enhances the storytelling in "Shutter Island. Scorsese employs quick cuts and jump cuts to present fragmented and fragmented memories. This editing style mirrors Teddy's fragmented state of mind and reinforces the sense of confusion and disorientation that permeates the film. By utilizing these editing techniques, Scorsese further immerses the audience into Teddy's unraveling psyche, intensifying the psychological thriller aspect of the story.

Furthermore, Scorsese's mise-en-scène choices greatly contribute to the storytelling in "Shutter Island. Scorsese meticulously crafts the set design and the positioning of the characters to heighten the sense of claustrophobia and paranoia. The dimly lit, cramped room in which the confrontation takes place creates a suffocating atmosphere, while the strategic placement of the characters within the frame enhances the psychological tension. Scorsese's meticulous attention to detail in the mise-en-scène elevates the storytelling and effectively conveys the oppressive and sinister nature of the institution. Through his use of visual symbolism, sound design, editing techniques, and meticulous mise-en-scène choices, Scorsese successfully immerses the audience into the nightmarish world of the film. His innovative approach to directing enhances the psychological thriller aspect of the story and keeps the viewers engaged and on the edge of their seats. Scorsese proves once again why he is considered one of the greatest directors of our time, and his directing style in "Shutter Island" is a testament to his unparalleled storytelling abilities

Chapter 6: Critical Analysis

- Discuss the reception of the movie by critics and audiences

The highly anticipated psychological thriller "Shutter Island," directed by Martin Scorsese and released in 2010, captivated audiences and critics alike. The film, based on the 2003 novel by Dennis Lehane, delves into the sinister world of a mental institution located on a remote island. In this chapter, we will explore the reception of the movie by both critics and audiences, examining their varied perspectives and interpretations.

Critics played a pivotal role in shaping the perception of "Shutter Island" among the general audience. The film garnered generally positive reviews, with many praising Scorsese's mastery of storytelling and his ability to immerse viewers in the twisted reality of the island. Critics applauded the film's cinematography, particularly the visually striking shots that conveyed the eerie atmosphere of the mental institution. Scorsese's choice of camera angles and lighting created a sense of unease, heightening the tension throughout the film.

Furthermore, the dynamic performances of the main cast received significant admiration from critics. Leonardo DiCaprio, who portrayed U. S. Marshal Teddy Daniels, delivered a captivating performance that showcased his versatility as an actor. His portrayal of Teddy's emotional and psychological turmoil was lauded as one of his most impressive performances to date. Similarly, Mark Ruffalo's portrayal of Teddy's partner, Chuck Aule, received accolades for its subtle nuances and strong chemistry with DiCaprio.

While critics generally responded positively to "Shutter Island," there were some who expressed reservations about the film's convoluted narrative. The intricate plot, which takes various unexpected twists and turns, left some viewers confused and frustrated. As a result, the film received criticism for being overly complex, making it inaccessible to a broader audience. Nonetheless, many critics appreciated Scorsese's adventurous approach, acknowledging that the complexity added an extra layer of intellectual engagement to the viewing experience.

Turning our attention to the audience reception, "Shutter Island" achieved considerable commercial success. The film resonated with the general public, becoming a box office hit and a popular topic for watercooler conversations. Audiences praised the intricacy of the plot, engaging in extensive discussions and theories about the true nature of the story. With its thought-provoking narrative, the film left a lasting impact on viewers and sparked conversations about identity, reality, and the nature of sanity.

The central themes explored in "Shutter Island" also resonated strongly with audiences. The film's examination of mental illness, manipulation, and the fragility of human perception struck a chord with viewers, prompting reflection and generating empathy towards the characters. The impact of these themes was further enhanced by Scorsese's meticulous attention to detail and his ability to evoke raw emotions, leading audiences to deepen their appreciation for the film.

Overall, the reception of "Shutter Island" by both critics and audiences was largely positive, despite some reservations expressed by a few. The film's ability to captivate viewers with its intriguing plot, stellar performances, and immersive cinematography solidified its position as a psychological thriller worth discussing and analyzing. Whether through the critical lens or the enthusiastic discussions among audiences, "Shutter Island" remained a film that resonated long after the credits rolled

- Analyze the themes and underlying messages of the film

In Martin Scorsese's film Shutter Island (2010), the director takes viewers on a harrowing journey into the depths of the human psyche. As a psychological thriller, the film explores several themes and underlying messages that contribute to its overall haunting atmosphere. Throughout the course of the movie, Scorsese masterfully weaves together elements of madness, guilt, perception, and the fragile nature of reality to create a thought-provoking cinematic experience.

One of the central themes in Shutter Island is madness. The film delves into the concept of insanity and the thin line that separates it from sanity. This theme is exemplified through the character of Teddy Daniels, played by Leonardo DiCaprio. As a U. S. Marshal investigating the disappearance of a patient at Ashecliffe Hospital, Teddy appears to be a rational and reliable protagonist. However, as the plot unravels, it becomes clear that Teddy himself is plagued by his own demons and struggles with his grip on reality. This exploration of madness serves as a reminder that the human mind can be a treacherous and enigmatic labyrinth, capable of distorting one's perception of the world around them.

Guilt is another prevalent theme in Shutter Island. The film examines the consequences of past actions and the psychological toll they can take on an individual. Teddy's involvement in the liberation of Dachau, a Nazi concentration camp, weighs heavily on his conscience. It haunts him, fueling his determination to uncover the truth behind the disappearance at Ashecliffe Hospital. Guilt becomes a driving force for Teddy, compelling him to confront his own demons and seek redemption. This exploration of guilt sends a powerful message about the lasting impact of one's past actions and the inner turmoil they can create.

Perception is also a crucial theme in Shutter Island. The film continuously blurs the line between what is real and what is imagined. Scorsese cleverly manipulates the viewers' perception through the use of distorted visuals, symbolic imagery, and unreliable narration. The audience is constantly engaged in questioning the authenticity of the events unfolding on screen, just as Teddy grapples with his own sense of reality. This exploration of perception reminds viewers of the fragility of their own perceptions and raises the question of what can be considered truly real in a world where reality can easily be distorted.

Beneath the surface, Shutter Island carries a deeper message about the nature of truth and the power of denial. The film reveals the dangers of burying painful memories and the lengths to which individuals will go to protect themselves from facing harsh realities. This underlying message aligns with the concept of psychological defense mechanisms, where people create elaborate illusions and delusions in order to shield themselves from painful truths. Scorsese's portrayal of denial in Shutter Island serves as a cautionary tale, highlighting the destructive consequences that can arise from denying one's own truth. Through the lenses of madness, guilt, perception, and denial, the film provides audiences with a harrowing experience that raises thought-provoking questions about the fragile nature of the human mind and the reality we construct for ourselves. By analyzing these themes and underlying messages, viewers are invited to delve into their own perceptions, confront their past actions, and contemplate the precarious balance between sanity and insanity. Shutter Island, as a psychological thriller, successfully captivates its audience through its masterful storytelling and thought-provoking themes, leaving a lasting impact on those who dare to unravel its intricacies

- Consider the film in the context of Scorsese's other works

Martin Scorsese's filmography is a treasure trove of cinematic brilliance, and his enthralling masterpiece, "Shutter Island" (2010), is no exception. As I delve into the depths of this psychological thriller, it becomes essential to consider the film in the context of Scorsese's other works. By doing so, we can uncover the thematic intricacies and technical finesse that epitomize Scorsese's directorial expertise.

One element that stands out when examining "Shutter Island" within the scope of Scorsese's filmography is his consistent exploration of the human psyche. Throughout his career, Scorsese has shown an unyielding fascination with the complexities of the human mind and the darkness that lurks within it. This thematic motif is beautifully exemplified in "Shutter Island," where the protagonist, U. S. Marshal Teddy Daniels, finds himself entangled in a web of psychological intrigue.

Similar to films such as "Taxi Driver" (1976) and "Raging Bull" (1980), Scorsese employs various visual and narrative techniques to immerse the audience in the deeply disturbed mindset of his protagonist. Through the use of distorted camera angles, eerie lighting, and disorienting editing, Scorsese creates a palpable sense of unease and paranoia. This technique, often referred to as "subjective cinematography," is a signature of Scorsese's directorial style, amplifying the immersive experience and blurring the boundaries between reality and illusion.

Furthermore, Scorsese's use of symbolism and recurrent themes in "Shutter Island" echoes his past work. Take, for instance, the recurring motif of water, which is a prevalent element in films like "Mean Streets" (1973) and "Gangs of New York" (2002). In "Shutter Island," water is not only a physical barrier, but it also symbolizes the depths of the human subconscious, mirroring the hidden truths that lie beneath the surface. Scorsese's adept use of symbolism not only enriches the narrative but also invites the viewer to delve deeper into the psychological complexities at play.

Additionally, when considering the film in the context of Scorsese's other works, it becomes apparent that "Shutter Island" shares similarities with his explorations of guilt and redemption. In films like "Goodfellas" (1990) and "The Departed" (2006), Scorsese delves into the morally ambiguous world of his characters, examining the consequences of their actions and their pursuit of atonement. This theme resonates strongly in "Shutter Island," where Teddy Daniels grapples with his own guilt and the possibility of redemption.

Scorsese's remarkable ability to craft complex and flawed characters is also showcased in "Shutter Island." Throughout his body of work, Scorsese has displayed a knack for bringing compelling characters to life, each with their own demons and intricacies. "Shutter Island" is no different, as we witness Teddy Daniels' haunting past and perpetually questioning his own sanity. Scorsese's consistent portrayal of flawed characters adds depth and relatability to his films, allowing the audience to forge a meaningful connection with the story on a personal level. By delving into the human psyche, utilizing visual and narrative techniques, employing symbolism, and delving into themes of guilt and redemption, Scorsese underscores his unwavering dedication to exploring the depths of the human condition. "Shutter Island" stands as a shining example of Scorsese's ability to captivate and challenge his audiences, solidifying his position as a true cinematic visionary

Chapter 7: Impact and Legacy

- Reflect on the lasting impact of "Shutter Island"

Reflecting on the lasting impact of "Shutter Island" is an intriguing endeavor, as director Martin Scorsese masterfully crafted a psychological thriller that continues to captivate audiences to this day. Released in 2010, the film presents a complex narrative that delves into the darkest recesses of the human mind, leaving a profound impact on viewers long after the credits roll.

One of the film's most enduring legacies lies in its exploration of the nature of reality and perception. Scorsese, known for his meticulous attention to detail, expertly blurs the lines between truth and illusion, continuously keeping audiences guessing. By weaving a story filled with twists and turns, the director forces viewers to question their own perceptions and confront the ambiguity of the human experience. This compelling examination of reality not only adds a layer of intrigue to the narrative but also encourages viewers to contemplate the fragility of their own sanity.

Furthermore, "Shutter Island" is notable for its nuanced portrayal of mental illness. The film takes place in a psychiatric institution, where main protagonist Teddy Daniels, portrayed brilliantly by Leonardo DiCaprio, investigates a disappearance that hides a much darker truth. Scorsese sensitively portrays the inner demons plaguing the characters, highlighting the delicate balance between sanity and madness. The lasting impact of this portrayal lies in its ability to shed light on the complexities of mental illness and raise awareness surrounding the stigmatization and misconceptions often associated with such conditions.

Another aspect of the lasting impact of "Shutter Island" is the film's cinematography and visual aesthetics. Scorsese, alongside his longtime collaborator, cinematographer Robert Richardson, creates a hauntingly beautiful atmosphere through the use of color palettes, composition, and a meticulous attention to detail. The hospital's stark and ominous interiors, juxtaposed with the chaotic and stormy surroundings, enhance the film's overall sense of unease and provide a visual representation of the characters' psychological turmoil. These visual choices not only heighten the suspense and tension but also leave a lasting imprint on viewers, immersing them in the unsettling world of "Shutter Island. ".

Moreover, the performances in "Shutter Island" contribute to its lasting impact. The film boasts a stellar ensemble cast, with standout performances from DiCaprio, Mark Ruffalo, and Ben Kingsley. DiCaprio's portrayal of Teddy Daniels is particularly poignant, as he expertly captures the character's internal struggle and vulnerability. His versatility as an actor shines through in his portrayal of a man haunted by his past and consumed by his quest for truth. The performances in "Shutter

Island" not only elevate the narrative but also leave a lasting impression on viewers, further solidifying the film's enduring legacy. Scorsese's creation remains a psychological thriller that challenges and engages viewers, leaving them pondering the boundaries of their own minds. The legacy of "Shutter Island" is undeniable, as it continues to be celebrated and analyzed as a masterclass in suspenseful storytelling and thought-provoking cinema

- Discuss its influence on the thriller genre

In Martin Scorsese's psychological thriller, "Shutter Island" (2010), the director's clever utilization of various cinematic techniques had a profound influence on the thriller genre. This unsettling film, adapted from Dennis Lehane's novel of the same name, perfectly encapsulates the essence of a psychological thriller, leaving the audience on the edge of their seats while challenging their notions of reality and truth. In this chapter, we will discuss the impact and legacy of "Shutter

Island" on the thriller genre, paving the way for future filmmakers to explore the depths of human psychology and push the boundaries of cinematic storytelling.

One of the most impactful aspects of "Shutter Island" is its meticulous attention to detail, particularly in its visual storytelling. Scorsese employs a mix of eerie lighting, haunting set designs, and atmospheric cinematography to create a constant sense of unease throughout the film. The island itself becomes a character, shrouded in mist, with its sinister cliffs and foreboding lighthouse. This attention to visual detail influenced subsequent thrillers, encouraging directors to use the environment as a means to create suspense and evoke emotions in the audience.

Furthermore, Scorsese's use of non-linear storytelling adds depth and complexity to the narrative. By interweaving flashbacks and unreliable character perspectives, "Shutter Island" blurs the lines between reality and illusion. This narrative technique effectively disorients the audience and immerses them in the unraveling mystery of the film. As a result, many contemporary thrillers have adopted similar non-linear structures to engage viewers and keep them guessing until the final revelation.

The performances in "Shutter Island" are another key element that influenced the thriller genre. Leonardo DiCaprio's portrayal of U. S. Marshal Teddy Daniels stands out as a tour de force performance. DiCaprio masterfully portrays the character's internal conflicts, grappling with grief, paranoia, and uncertainty, which simultaneously captivates and confounds the audience. This multi-layered characterization of the protagonist significantly influenced future thrillers, encouraging actors to explore complex psychological landscapes within their roles.

Equally important is the film's chilling score, composed by Robbie Robertson. The haunting melodies and dissonant tones elevate the tension and unease experienced by the audience. It is no coincidence that many subsequent thrillers have sought to replicate the atmospheric quality of "Shutter Island" through the strategic use of soundscapes and scores that heighten suspense and unnerving emotions.

Another innovative aspect of "Shutter Island" is its exploration of psychological themes and the nature of identity. The film delves into the darkest corners of the human mind, touching on topics such as trauma, cognition, and perception. By utilizing psychopathology as a central driving force, "Shutter Island" laid the groundwork for a new breed of psychological thrillers that delve into the complexities of the human psyche, challenging audiences to question their own perceptions of reality.

The lasting influence of "Shutter Island" can be seen in the evolution of the thriller genre, which has increasingly embraced complex narratives, atmospheric visuals, and thought-provoking themes. With its stunning artistry, indelible performances, and a narrative that keeps viewers guessing until the final frame, "Shutter Island" set a new standard for psychological thrillers. It paved the way for filmmakers to experiment with structure, challenge conventions, and explore the darkest aspects of the human psyche. Its legacy continues to resonate, inspiring future generations of filmmakers to delve deep into the realms of psychological suspense, ensuring the genre's perpetuity. Martin Scorsese's meticulous attention to detail, non-linear storytelling, exceptional performances, haunting score, and exploration of psychological themes have left an indelible mark on the genre. The film's influence can be seen in subsequent thrillers, which continue to push boundaries and captivate audiences with their ability to engage, unsettle, and challenge our perceptions of reality

- Consider the film's place in cinematic history

Shutter Island, directed by Martin Scorsese and released in 2010, holds a significant place in cinematic history. This psychological thriller serves as a thought-provoking commentary on various elements of storytelling, filmmaking techniques, and the impact of psychological narratives on cinema. By exploring themes of identity, paranoia, and the human psyche, Shutter Island has left a lasting legacy and continues to impact the cinematic landscape.

One of the notable aspects of Shutter Island is its narrative structure, which challenges conventional storytelling techniques. Scorsese employs a non-linear approach, blurring the line between reality and delusion. This approach heightens the suspense and keeps the audience engaged, while also reflecting the fragmented state of the protagonist's mind. This experimental narrative structure not only adds layers of complexity to the film but also showcases Scorsese's innovative approach to storytelling.

Furthermore, Shutter Island delves into the psychology of its characters, particularly the protagonist, Teddy Daniels. The film explores the themes of trauma, memory, and the unreliability of perception. As the audience is taken on a journey through Teddy's distorted reality, it raises questions regarding the nature of truth and the boundaries between sanity and madness. Scorsese's meticulous attention to detail in portraying the psychological state of the characters adds to the film's impact and legacy, as it showcases the power of cinema as a medium to delve into the depths of the human mind.

Another key element of Shutter Island's impact on cinematic history lies in its cinematography and visual style. The film features stunning visuals that amplify the psychological tension and create an unsettling atmosphere. Scorsese utilizes various visual techniques, such as the use of shadows, vast landscapes, and hauntingly beautiful imagery, to immerse the audience into the eerie world of Shutter Island. These striking visuals contribute to the film's thematic exploration and make it a visually captivating viewing experience.

Additionally, the performances in Shutter Island further solidify its place in cinematic history. Leonardo DiCaprio delivers a compelling and nuanced portrayal of Teddy Daniels, captivating the audience with his emotional intensity. His performance showcases his versatility as an actor and adds another layer of depth to the film's impact. Alongside DiCaprio, the supporting cast, including Mark Ruffalo, Ben Kingsley, and Michelle Williams, deliver equally stellar performances that contribute to the film's overall success.

Moreover, Shutter Island pays homage to various cinematic genres and influences, reminding audiences of its position within cinematic history. Scorsese incorporates elements of film noir, neo-noir, and psychological thrillers into the narrative, enriching the film's depth and creating a multidimensional viewing experience. This homage not only showcases Scorsese's extensive knowledge and appreciation of film history but also places Shutter Island within a lineage of influential cinematic works. Martin Scorsese's directorial prowess, combined with a thought-provoking screenplay and meticulous attention to detail, has solidified this psychological thriller as a lasting contribution to the cinematic landscape. Shutter Island continues to captivate audiences, challenging

their perceptions and leaving a lasting impact on the
history of cinema

Conclusion

- *Summarize key points discussed in the book*

By dissecting the various thematic motifs and character dynamics, the book unravels the psychological complexities that lie at the heart of this gripping thriller. Throughout the film, the line between reality and illusion, sanity and insanity, becomes increasingly blurred. By exploring the psychological fractures and traumas experienced by the characters, Scorsese illuminates the fragile nature of the human psyche and the profound impact it can have on one's perception of reality.

Another key point discussed in the book is the exploration of power dynamics and manipulation. Cawley, the enigmatic psychiatrist. It becomes apparent throughout the narrative that Teddy is both a pawn and a manipulator in this psychological game, adding an additional layer of complexity to his quest for the truth. Scorsese skillfully portrays the shifting power dynamics, leaving the audience questioning the true intentions and motivations of each character. Through haunting flashbacks and the exploration of Teddy's past, the film delves into the depths of post-traumatic stress disorder and the haunting power of guilt. Scorsese masterfully captures the nuances of guilt and trauma, weaving them seamlessly into the narrative to create a hauntingly gripping atmosphere. The isolated asylum becomes more than just a backdrop; it becomes a metaphorical embodiment of the characters' mental states. Scorsese's attention to detail in creating a dark and foreboding environment adds an eerie sense of unease, enhancing the psychological impact of the story. " Through the exploration of themes such as duality, power dynamics, guilt, and trauma, the book sheds light on the psychological complexities that underlie this thrilling narrative

- Reflect on the significance of "Shutter Island" as a psychological thriller

"Shutter Island" is more than just your typical psychological thriller. Directed by the brilliant Martin Scorsese, this film delves deep into the realm of the human psyche, weaving a complex narrative filled with intrigue, suspense, and a sense of constant unease. In this essay, we will reflect on the significance of "Shutter Island" as a psychological thriller, uncovering the intricacies and layers that make this film an intense and thought-provoking experience.

First and foremost, the setting of "Shutter Island" plays a crucial role in its portrayal as a psychological thriller. The isolated and foreboding atmosphere of the titular island sets the stage for the unraveling of the protagonist's fragile mental state. The desolate landscapes, gothic architecture, and stormy weather all contribute to a sense of claustrophobia and suspense, leading the audience into a state of unease. The island itself becomes a character, an entity with its own secrets and mysteries waiting to be discovered or buried.

Furthermore, "Shutter Island" explores the concept of madness and the fragile nature of the mind. The narrative revolves around Teddy Daniels, a U. S. Marshal assigned to investigate the disappearance of a female patient from Ashecliffe Hospital, a psychiatric facility on the island. As the plot progresses, we become immersed in Teddy's own struggle with reality, questioning what is real and what is merely a construct of his own troubled mind. This constant blurring of lines between perception and hallucination keeps the audience on the edge of their seats, constantly second-guessing their own understanding of the story.

The film's exploration of psychological trauma and its lasting effects also adds to its significance as a psychological thriller. Teddy's past experiences as a World War II veteran and his personal tragedies are seamlessly interwoven into the narrative, providing a deep and personal connection to his descent into madness. Through flashbacks and haunting memories, we witness the emotional scars that haunt Teddy and how they come to the forefront of his mind on Shutter Island. This portrayal of trauma and its impact on the human psyche adds a layer of complexity and psychological depth to the film, elevating it from a mere suspenseful thriller to a thought-provoking examination of the human condition.

Another aspect that contributes to the significance of "Shutter Island" as a psychological thriller is the masterful use of symbolism and visual storytelling. Scorsese employs visual motifs such as water, fire, and clocks throughout the film to represent the passage of time, the cyclical nature of Teddy's memories, and the overwhelming presence of guilt and remorse. These symbolic elements not only enhance the visual appeal of the film but also serve as powerful psychological triggers, heightening the audience's emotional response and immersing them further into the story. Through its atmospheric setting, exploration of the complexities of the human mind, depiction of psychological trauma, and masterful use of symbolism and visual storytelling, this film transcends the boundaries of the genre, prompting us to reflect on the fragility of our own sanity. Martin Scorsese's "Shutter Island" is a true cinematic masterpiece, leaving a lasting impact on both the mind and the emotions of its audience

- Offer final thoughts on the film's enduring appeal and cultural relevance

In the final analysis, it is undeniable that Martin Scorsese's film, Shutter Island (2010), possesses an enduring appeal and cultural relevance that has helped it to become a psychological thriller of significant and lasting impact. This essay will delve into the depths of Shutter Island's enduring appeal and cultural relevance, elucidating the various elements that contribute to its enduring popularity and its ability to captivate audiences.

One of the key factors that contribute to Shutter Island's enduring appeal is its masterful storytelling. From the very beginning, Scorsese skillfully weaves a web of suspense and mystery that keeps the audience on the edge of their seats throughout the film. The intricate plot, filled with unexpected twists and turns, grabs hold of the viewer's attention and refuses to let go. Scorsese's meticulous attention to detail, combined with his impeccable pacing, creates an atmosphere of tension and unease that lingers long after the credits roll.

Furthermore, the film's exploration of psychological trauma and the human mind adds another layer of depth to its enduring appeal and cultural relevance. Shutter Island delves into the darkest recesses of the human psyche, exposing the inherent vulnerabilities and complexities that exist within all of us. Through the character of Teddy Daniels, expertly portrayed by Leonardo DiCaprio, the film explores the effects of trauma on the human mind and raises thought-provoking questions about the nature of memory, perception, and identity.

Additionally, Shutter Island's cultural relevance stems from its commentary on the nature of power and the abuse of authority. Set in the 1950s, a period marked by a growing awareness of the dangers of unchecked authority, the film serves as a cautionary tale about the potential for corruption and manipulation within institutions of power. Scorsese, through his depiction of the sinister practices at Shutter Island's Ashecliffe Hospital, shines a light on the ethical dilemmas that arise when power is concentrated in the hands of a few.

Moreover, the film's exploration of mental illness and the stigmatization associated with it resonates with contemporary societal concerns. Shutter Island challenges the conventional narratives surrounding mental illness and highlights the need for empathy and understanding in our interactions with individuals who are suffering. By humanizing characters plagued by mental illness, Scorsese not only creates a sense of empathy in the audience but also sparks a larger conversation about the treatment and perception of individuals with mental health disorders. Martin Scorsese's film stands as a testament to the power of cinema to captivate and provoke thought, engaging audiences on both an intellectual and emotional level. Whether it is the skillfully crafted suspense, the complex portrayal of the human mind, or the social commentary that resonates with contemporary concerns, Shutter Island continues to hold a prominent place in the annals of psychological thrillers. Its enduring appeal and cultural relevance ensure that it will be analyzed, discussed, and appreciated for years to come

Made in the USA
Monee, IL
30 November 2024

71594586R00053